Written by Louisa Somerville
Designed by Louise Morley

First edition for the United States, the Philippines, and Puerto Rico,
published 1997 by Barron's Educational Series, Inc.

Text © HarperCollins Publishers Ltd 1996
Illustrations © HarperCollins Publishers Ltd 1996
Published by arrangement with HarperCollins Publishers Ltd

The author/illustrator asserts the moral right to be
identified as the author/illustrator of this work.

Illustrations: Charlotte Hard
Photographs: Ardea: 24, /L Bomford 25 /P Morris 26;
BBC Natural History Unit/J Foott 34; Bruce Coleman Ltd:
/J Johnson 43, /L Lee Rue, /E Pott 42, /H Reinhard 54t;
NHPA: /B & C Alexander 8/9, /Agence Nature 55, /A.N.T. 16, 22, 30,
31, 48, /H Ausloos 54b, 59, /A Bannister 19, 57, /G Bernard 23,
/M Danegger 50b, /M Harvey 36b, /B Hawkes 10, 13, /D Heuclin
20, 28, 29, /N Dennis 18, /E A Janes 12, 15, 40b, 52t, /B Jones &
M Shimlock 17, /D Karp 35, 50t, /R Kirchner 8, 38b, /T Kitchin &
V Hurst 38t, 39, /S Kraseman 52b, 53, /G Lacz 5, 32t, 36t, 37t, 40t,
/Y Lanceau 56, 58, /S Robinson 32b, 46, 47, 61, /A Rouse 14, 41, /J
Sauvanet 21, /K Schafer 44, /J Shaw 51, /E Soder 11; Oxford Scientific
Films: /M Fogden 23, /R Kuiter 27, /T McHugh 49, /K Ringland 57.

All inquiries should be addressed to:
Barron's Educational Series, Inc.
250 Wireless Boulevard
Hauppauge, New York 11788

ISBN 0-7641-5037-5

Library of Congress Catalog Card Number: 97-70523

Printed in Hong Kong
987654321

Baby
Animals

BARRON'S

CONTENTS

BABIES BORN FROM EGGS

Penguin 8

Ostrich 10

Cuckoo 12

Owl 14

Turtle 16

Crocodile 18

Snake 20

Frog 22

Fish 24

Sea Horse 26

Spider and Scorpion 28

BABY MAMMALS

Dolphin 30

Hippopotamus 32

Beaver 34

Polar Bear 36

Grizzly Bear 38

Tiger 40

Giraffe 42

Elephant 44

Chimpanzee 46

Koala and Kangaroo 48

Fox 50

Deer 52

Horse 54

Cat 56

Dog 58

Index 60

PENGUIN

An Adélie penguin with her two young chicks

Penguins live in the bitterly cold Antarctic. The mother penguin comes ashore to lay a single egg, which she passes to the father before returning to the ocean. The father penguin balances the egg on his feet and covers it with a flap of skin on his belly to keep it warm. When the chick hatches, it's covered with thick

down like a big fur coat. The young penguin won't be able to swim until it has lost its down and grown waterproof adult feathers.

In spring the female emperor penguin returns from the water to feed her chick, which soon learns to beg for food from its mother.

OSTRICH

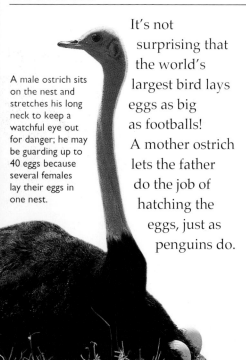

A male ostrich sits on the nest and stretches his long neck to keep a watchful eye out for danger; he may be guarding up to 40 eggs because several females lay their eggs in one nest.

It's not surprising that the world's largest bird lays eggs as big as footballs! A mother ostrich lets the father do the job of hatching the eggs, just as penguins do.

An ostrich chick has striped brown feathers to keep it hidden when it is lying on the ground.

When it is hatched, the baby chick looks around for the nearest big, moving object. This tends to be the parent bird, fortunately! The chick remembers the bird's shape, and then follows it everywhere. This behavior is known as imprinting.

CUCKOO

A newly hatched cuckoo in another bird's nest

Some mother cuckoos lay their egg in another bird's nest. After the cuckoo chick hatches, it takes each of the other eggs on its back in turn and hurls them out of the nest. The baby cuckoo then has the nest to itself. Thus, it gets all the food from its new parents who feed the cuckoo chick as if it was their own. It grows very fast and soon fills the whole nest. After about three weeks, the cuckoo is ready to leave the nest and flies away.

OWL

As soon as a mother owl lays her first egg, she sits on it to keep it warm. This egg is the first to hatch because it starts growing before the others. By the time the last baby owlet hatches, the oldest is already two weeks old. The mother feeds the owlets with tiny bits of meat.

A tawny owl and her chick, which now has most of its adult feathers

If food is scarce, only the oldest owlets get enough to survive. Owlets are born nearly naked and huddle together for warmth. In a short time they are covered with soft down. After a few weeks their adult feathers begin to grow through the down and soon the owlets are "fully fledged."

A pair of barn owl chicks covered with down

Tawny owlets nestling in a tree trunk

TURTLE

Most turtles go ashore to lay their eggs in holes in the sand. Just before it hatches, the young turtle grows a sharp tooth, called an

A newly hatched green turtle and its egg

egg tooth, on its snout. It uses the tooth to slit open the shell. Soon after it has hatched, the egg tooth drops off. As dusk falls, the young turtles make a dash for their home in the sea. It is a dangerous trip, as crabs and seabirds are waiting on the shore for a juicy turtle meal.

16

CROCODILE

A mother crocodile takes good care
of her young. She makes a nest for
her eggs on land and guards them
until they hatch. The newly hatched
babies call out to their mother.
Then she gently picks them up in
her mouth and carries them to a

A female Nile crocodile carrying
her newly hatched babies from
the nest to the water

A Nile crocodile uses its egg tooth to break through the brittle shell.

quiet pool. She has a special pocket in the bottom of her mouth where she can hold about six youngsters at a time. The mother stays with her young crocodiles for a few months to protect them until they are old enough to fend for themselves.

SNAKE

A grass snake laying her eggs

A baby grass snake hatching

Some snakes lay their eggs in a warm nest of rotting plants, while others make a nest underground. Some even build a mound of twigs to protect the eggs. A grass snake does not lay her eggs in the grass; she chooses a sandy or mossy spot. The mother curls around her eggs to keep them warm with her own body.

Young emerald tree boas look just like their parents, except that they are dull brown instead of brilliant green.

She sometimes stays like this for two months and doesn't eat. Baby snakes look after themselves as soon as they are hatched – and that includes being able to bite!

FROG

Platypus frogs hatch from eggs inside the mother's stomach; you can see just how tiny the baby frog is next to this paperclip.

A frog starts life as a tadpole. A tadpole has only a tiny head and tail and doesn't look at all like a frog. Most tadpoles feed on the yolk of

A tree frog's spawn dangles from a branch overhanging the water; as the tadpoles hatch, they fall into the water below.

the egg from which they were born. Later they eat weeds, insects, and worms. About seven weeks after hatching, the tadpoles begin to grow back legs. Then they grow front legs and absorb their tails. Now they look more like frogs! Soon they will be ready to leave the water and explore their new home on land.

A male poison arrow frog carrying eggs on his back

FISH

A male three-spined stickleback guarding his nest

The male stickleback is a full-time
father. First he builds a nest of
weeds. The female lays her eggs
inside the nest and swims away.
The father fertilizes the eggs, then
guards the nest and looks after the

24

babies when they hatch.

Unlike stickleback babies, most young fish, known as fry, stay with their mother. Some mother fish even carry their babies inside their mouth. The mother will let her babies out to feed in safety but if an enemy comes too close, she quickly sucks them in again.

A female Lake Malawi fish from Africa, blowing her fry out of her mouth

SEA HORSE

Sea horses are the only animals to be born from a father. A female sea horse squirts her eggs into a pouch on the male's belly. The male keeps the eggs safe for about a month, until it is time for the babies to hatch. He wraps his tail around a piece of seaweed to anchor himself. Then up to 200 tiny sea horses shoot out of his belly. The babies look just like their parents, but they're only about $\frac{1}{16}$ of an inch (1 mm) long!

A male sea horse giving birth

SPIDER AND SCORPION

A wolf spider carrying a large load of spiderlings

A hundred or so baby wolf spiderlings climb out of a cocoon under their mother's belly and scuttle onto her back, where they cling to her hairy body. As the spiderlings grow, their skin gets tighter and tighter until they molt, meaning they shed their skin. When their new skin gets too tight, they molt again. After this, the spiderlings are big enough to leave their mother's back.

Newborn scorpions also climb onto their mother's back when they hatch. They hold on tightly with their tiny claws. The poisonous sting at the tip of the mother's tail is enough warning to her enemies for the babies to be safe from attack.

A female scorpion carrying her young

DOLPHIN

A young dolphin leaping

Mammal babies do not hatch from eggs. They grow inside their mother and when they are born she feeds them with her own milk. As soon as a baby dolphin is born, its mother pushes it onto her back and lifts it up toward the surface of the water to gulp air through its blowhole. The mother feeds her baby by squirting rich, thick milk into its mouth. The baby may stay with its mother for several years.

A mother and baby dolphin swimming side by side

HIPPOPOTAMUS

A pygmy hippo is unusual because she gives birth to her calf on land.

A baby hippopotamus (called a calf) is usually born in the water. The hippo calf soon learns to swim alongside its mother. It stays close to its mother so she can protect it with

This hippo is being bottle-fed because it has lost its mother.

her large body and huge teeth. When the mother is swimming in deep water, she will carry her baby on her head. Young hippos live in special nursery groups with other mothers and calves. The females often babysit for each other. If one mother goes off to feed or mate, another one will look after her calf.

A hippo and her calf wallowing in the water

BEAVER

Beavers raise their families in a den, called a lodge. The lodge is in a dam of logs built across a stream by the beavers. Each spring, a mother beaver gives birth to two or three babies, known as kits, in the lodge.

Kits are excellent swimmers. They use their webbed back feet to paddle.

They steer with their broad, flat tail. If a kit is in danger, its mother may lift it up in her front paws and run with it to safety.

Above: A beaver kit on land

Left: A mother beaver feeding with her baby in shallow water

35

POLAR BEAR

In winter, a mother polar bear digs a den under the snow to make a sheltered place where she can have her babies. Polar bears are the only type of bear cubs to be born with fur. The cubs lie on their mother's belly to keep warm. In spring, the mother breaks open the sealed den with her paw.

A cub at the edge of the ice waiting for a catch

The cubs follow her outside. Their oily fur and a layer of fat below the skin keep them warm in the icy

Mother and baby playing

water while they learn to swim. The mother teaches her cubs to trap and kill seals. She waits for a seal to come up for air. When its head pops up, she stuns it with a blow from her paw.

GRIZZLY BEAR

A bear cub eating berries

Like polar bears, grizzly bear cubs are born in a den in the middle of winter. The mother grizzly and her cubs leave the den in the spring. The cubs

Right: A young grizzly in the Rocky Mountains

Left: A mother playing with her two cubs

start to explore. They climb trees and wrestle with each other. The mother teaches her cubs how to catch fish to eat. They watch as she stands in a shallow river. When a fish swims by, she grabs it in her huge paw.

TIGER

A tiger cub soon learns how effective a warning snarl can be.

A Siberian tiger carrying her cub to safety

Tiger cubs are born in a den hidden beneath a fallen tree or some rocks. At first they are completely helpless, relying on their mother to feed and look after them. But they soon begin to explore. Like other young meat-eaters, tiger cubs spend lots of time playing.

They stalk and pounce on each other, which builds up their muscles and teaches them how to be good at catching prey. If her cubs are in danger, a mother tiger will carry them to safety, holding them gently in her strong jaws.

The stripes on these two Bengal tiger cubs help to camouflage them in long grass.

GIRAFFE

A young giraffe drinks milk from a nipple between its mother's back legs.

A newborn giraffe has a long drop into the world because giraffes give birth standing up. The baby is born feet first and falls 5.3 feet (1.6 m) to the ground. Within a few minutes it can stand up; it is walking and running by the time it's a few hours old. The baby giraffe is already 6.6 feet (2 m) tall – which is taller than most adult humans. At first the baby drinks only its

mother's milk. Soon, however, the young giraffe learns to stretch up its long neck and strip leaves off the trees with its tongue. Adult giraffes sleep standing up, but a baby curls up on the ground to sleep, watched over by its mother.

ELEPHANT

A few hours after it is born, a baby elephant, called a calf, is ready to follow the herd. If the calf gets tired, it hangs onto its mother's tail with its trunk. It can already smell, feel, and breathe through its trunk, but it

An adult African elephant and calf enjoying a drink at a watering hole

may take months
to learn to use its
trunk for drinking
and washing.
Until then the calf
sucks up water
with its mouth.
It learns to use its
trunk for many
other things too,
such as tearing
leaves off trees

A calf following closely
behind its mother

and lifting branches. An elephant
calf stays with its mother until it is
about 10 or 12 years old, longer than
any other animal, except humans.

CHIMPANZEE

This young chimp is learning to hold a twig.

To young chimpanzees, the forest is just a big playground! They swing through the branches and climb tree trunks and vines, all of which strengthens their arm muscles. Chimps need strong arms to build a leafy nest of twigs and branches to sleep in each night. Young chimps watch their parents closely to see how they use sticks to dig insects out of the ground.

A young chimp grooms an older female chimp.

KOALA AND KANGAROO

Koalas, like kangaroos, live in Australia.

A koala is a marsupial, an animal that has a special pouch for carrying its baby. When the young koala leaves its mother's

Koala mother and baby

pouch, it rides around on her back until it is old enough to look after itself. A kangaroo is another marsupial. At birth the baby, called a joey, is no bigger than a grape. The joey

A young joey spends time outside the pouch, but leaps back in for a meal or to hide from danger.

drinks milk from nipples inside the mother's pouch. After a few months it will hop out of the pouch and start to explore.

FOX

A cub drinking

Fox cubs are born in a den. It may be under a fallen tree, in shrubs, or in the deserted den of another

Red fox cubs sniffing the air outside their den, their pricked-up ears are alert to the smallest sounds.

animal, such as a badger or rabbit. The growing cubs soon start to play outside the den. They play chasing and wrestling games, which

An Arctic fox cub looking for shelter during a storm

teach them hunting skills. The cubs are safe because their mother will bark to warn them of danger. If a cub gets lost, it yelps until its mother finds it. Arctic foxes have dark fur in the summer but have a white coat in the winter so that they can hunt without being seen in the snow.

DEER

A young fawn asleep in the undergrowth

A baby fallow deer drinks milk from its mother.

A young deer, called a fawn, is born in a patch of undergrowth in the spring. For the first few days the fawn stays alone in its birthplace. Its spotted coat helps it to stay hidden from its enemies. The mother comes only to nurse it. She approaches cautiously to avoid drawing the attention of enemies to her newborn

A white-tailed deer sniffing her fawn's hind legs;
she knows it is her baby because it shares her scent.

fawn. Within a few days, mother
and baby join the herd. They will
always recognize each other because
they share exactly the same scent.
In a few months the fawn loses its
spotted coat. Now that it can run fast,
it doesn't need to be so well hidden.

HORSE

When a baby horse, called a foal, is born, its mother licks it to make it clean and dry, and to start its breathing.

A mare with her new foal

A wild mare and foal on moorland in France

Right: A foal trotting with its mother

Unlike many mammal babies, it can already see, hear, and smell. As soon as it is born, the foal staggers to its feet and drinks milk from its mother. After three months it begins to eat grass. The young foal stays close to the mare, and if it's frightened, it will hide under her.

CAT

A newborn kitten spends its time sleeping or drinking milk from a nipple on its mother's belly. A kitten is born with its eyes closed, but they will open after about a week. Like human babies, kittens' eyes are blue at first and slowly change color.

An Abyssinian
cat and kitten

The mother carries her kittens, taking them gently by the scruff of their necks with her teeth. After three weeks, a kitten is ready to take its first steps. A cat is

A tabby kitten

a member of the same animal family as a tiger, so when a kitten plays it is in fact learning how to stalk and catch prey, as a tiger cub does. A kitten will lie in wait to pounce on a piece of string, just as it will pounce on a mouse when it is older.

57

DOG

A cuddly puppy

Newborn puppies
drink their
mother's milk but
they soon need
more solid food.
The mother can
provide this for
her puppies
by throwing
up after she
has chewed and swallowed a meal
of meat. After about nine days,
puppies open their eyes for the first
time. Puppies need plenty of exercise
in order to grow properly and they
love to play with each other.

A mother guarding her puppy!

INDEX

Beaver 34–35

Cat 56–57

Chimpanzee 46–47

Crocodile 18–19

Cuckoo 12–13

Deer 52–53

Dog 58–59

Dolphin 30–31

Elephant 44–45

Fish 24–25

Fox 50–51

Frog 22–23

Giraffe 42–43

Grizzly bear 38–39

Hippopotamus 32–33

Horse 54–55

Kangaroo 48–49

Koala 48–49

Ostrich 10–11

Owl 14–15

Penguin 8–9

Polar bear 36–37

Scorpion 28–29

Sea horse 26–27

Snake 20–21

Spider 28–29

Tiger 40–41

Turtle 16–17